Wayward Journey

Richard H. Arakawa

ASPECT Books
www.ASPECTBooks.com

World rights reserved. This book or any portion thereof may not be copied or reproduced in any form or manner whatever, except as provided by law, without the written permission of the publisher, except by a reviewer who may quote brief passages in a review.

This book is sold with the understanding that the publisher is not engaged in giving spiritual, legal, medical, or other professional advice. If authoritative advice is needed, the reader should seek the counsel of a competent professional.

Copyright © 2012 Aspect Books
ISBN-13: 978-1-57258-862-4 (Paperback)
ISBN-13: 978-1-57258-863-2 (ePub)
ISBN-13: 978-1-57258-864-0 (Kindle/Mobi)

Library of Congress Control Number: 2012945866

Published by

ASPECT Books

www.ASPECTBooks.com

Table of Contents

Introduction v

Chapter 1   The Early Years 7

Chapter 2   Remarriage and Adoption 11

Chapter 3   Good Memories 15

Chapter 4   Other Memories 24

Chapter 5   Life Changing Events 29

Chapter 6   College Days 41

Chapter 7   Important Lessons From College 53

Chapter 8   Places and Persons 59

Chapter 9   Calm and Turmoil 73

Chapter 10   Addicted 81

Chapter 11   Angels 88

Chapter 12   Other Encounters 92

Chapter 13   Not Just Incidents 98

Chapter 14   Binding 104

Introduction

Life is sometimes compared to a continually flowing river. Whether our lives may be comparable to a mighty river is arguable. Some of us would be better being an unknown stream that joins a mighty river somewhere along its pathway. Without streams, some rivers may not be so mighty. Some rivers might eventually no longer exist.

Sometimes the course may be straight, smooth, and steady. At other times, it might be filled with twists and turns, rough or smooth spots, fast or slow sections, but regardless of the changes, it still moves toward the river that it contributes to. Though sometimes well-known while at other times unknown and apparently insignificant, each stream is important.

Our own life may seem insignificant. We may not know all the particulars about where we were born, what life was like during our early years, or the many details that contribute to making us who we are today. But an unseen Person is there with us, working on our behalf. When things are rough and unexpected turns challenge us, hope arises by intervention, sometimes truly divine, at other times by the ministry of other people who God provides for our benefit. Whether young or old, we all have a life story that can lead us and others to have hope in Jesus, now and for eternity.

This is a story of a life filled with twists and turns, smooth and rough courses. This is the story of a life journey that will hopefully continue in eternity with our Lord and Redeemer.

Names have been changed to protect those involved. Some readers may find some of the details troubling. But these details are written as part of the "rough" parts of this journey. Ronald, the primary character, is called Hide-chan in the early part of his life. This is not fiction. It is a true story. The experiences and illustrations in this book were written in hopes that readers will think about just how much God cares for us and gives us hope.

Chapter 1

The Early Years

January 26, 1945. World War II was still in progress. The fighting was bitter between the Allies and the Axis. Great sacrifices were made by all countries involved in this great conflict. Hope and despair were not far separated in such times.

Hope was high for Kimi-chan and Yukio-san as they welcomed their newborn son six weeks earlier. It made the cold winter nights just a little warmer for this poor couple.

But tragedy was to strike this couple not long after hope was kindled in their hearts. Yukio-san died soon after the birth of his son. Kimi-chan became a widow, and their son, Hide-chan, became fatherless. The exact details of Yukio-san's death are somewhat unknown, but he was a carpenter, and he died as a result of an industrial accident at work.

Life became even more difficult for Kimi-chan after her husband's death. She now had the challenge of raising a son and being able to meet the daily necessities of life, such as a place to live, enough food for the two of them, and clothing.

The good Lord, in His infinite mercy, heard the pleas of a very desperate mother and provided for her and her son. She did struggle, as one can imagine, living in post-war Japan. But a kind lady came into the picture. She helped to provide for this fatherless family as best she could, making personal sacrifices for them. She took care of them until Kimi-chan was able to work as a street peddler selling small household goods.

Kimi-chan worked and took care of Hide-chan by carrying him on her back as she peddled her goods on the streets of Osaka. The unnamed "aunt" made sure they had food and clothing. She was an angel in human form. Her kindness and caring attitude were a lifesaver!

Hide-chan has two memories stored in the hallways of his mind from these early years. The first is an image of him strapped to his mother's back returning from a hard days work. His tired mother is greeted by the "aunt" in a very gracious manner. The other is similar. He is older and the "aunt" is watching him while his mother works. He remembers the "aunt" greeting his mother

The Early Years

with kindness and respect as she returned from her hard day at work.

Perhaps, Hide-chan will meet this "aunt" again in the new earth, since he has not had the opportunity to do so since Kimi-

No one expected things to happen the way they did.

chan and he left Japan so many years ago.

In August of 1945 Japan's World War II endeavors ended. Japan surrendered to the Allies, and placed their fate in the hands of the United States of America. This was providential. This helped Japan recover from the devastation and ruin caused by the war, especially after the atomic bombs were dropped on Hiroshima and Nagasaki. In the end, Japan rose out of the ruins to become a global economic power.

The end of the war was important for Kimi-chan and Hide-chan as well. It made it easier for Kimi-chan to return to Hawaii with her young son. Not much is known about the process she went through to get the proper paperwork completed, but she finally worked things out to return to Hawaii. You see, Kimi-chan was born on the island of Hawaii to immigrant plantation workers. But she later attended school in Japan where she later met and married Yukio-san. One of Kimi-chan's aunts described Yukio-san as a nice, kind, hardworking man. No one expected things to happen the way they did.

After much hard work and dedication to her young son, Kimi-chan arrived in Honolulu harbor when Hide-chan was about 3 years old. The two of them were met by Kimi-chan's mother, two uncles and aunts, and a cousin. The tired mother and son arrived on President Lines. This was by no means like taking a pleasure cruise on today's modern cruise lines. But it was the best way to travel between Hawaii and Japan for the less fortunate in the late 1940s and early 1950s.

Chapter 2

Remarriage and Adoption

Parents do the best they can for their children no matter how difficult the circumstances may be. In Kimi-chan's case she chose to remarry to provide for Hide-chan. Koji-san was a poor poultry farmer who she met through a neighbor. Upon getting married, they moved to Waialae, where many other farmers of primarily Japanese-American descent lived on leased lands from the Bishop Estates. Some of the residents became building contractors but were still allowed to live on the leased properties.

Life on the farm was a challenge. Chicken feed and restocking chicks was costly. Profit margins were very low, if at all profitable. But they scraped by and managed to provide for the little family. Of course, things became more difficult when in the summer of 1951 a newborn was added to the family. But despite the difficulty, baby Dawn's arrival was a somewhat joyous event.

Unfortunately, Hide-chan had an accident that same summer. He was playing at a neighbor's place with two of his friends when they decided to rest after playing in the heat. The three friends looked for a good place to rest. It was then that they spotted a cement/concrete mixing box leaning against the wall of an open storage building. So the three boys decided to sit on the bottom of the box, with Hide-chan in the middle. This caused the box to tip over and come crashing to the ground! The two boys sitting on the ends ran, one to the left and one to the right. They escaped injury, but Hide-chan ran straight ahead. The box fell and broke his leg.

So it was that Hide-chan ended up in the hospital at the same time his sister was born. Fortunately, his leg healed, and he was able to walk and run with his friends once again.

On another occasion, Hide-chan had another brush with disaster. He liked playing ball. One day he went to see if his friends were home to play ball with, but they weren't. So he decided to toss the ball in the air and play catch by himself. He was so engrossed in his play that, unfortunately, he ran out into the street in front of his friends' home to catch the ball and was hit by a car. Fortunately for all involved, he was not hurt, because the driver was driving very slowly on their country road. The driver immediately stopped and made sure that Hide-chan was okay. Hide-chan was eventually legally adopted by his stepfather and

... *life is not always ideal.*

became a naturalized citizen of the United States of America. It was at this time that he was given an English name—Ronald.

Since his new father came from a fairly large family, Ronald's family suddenly became larger. Ronald's stepfather had five brothers and one sister, and there were several older cousins.

Although he was received fairly well by his new family, there were some who did not treat him kindly. Sometimes acceptance of others is immediate and spontaneous. Sometimes it is a slow process, and sometimes it does not happen at all. In Ronald's case, all of his extended family eventually accepted him.

Remarriage and adoption can be good things, but they can also be very difficult for all involved. If things go smoothly, without added financial burdens or relationship problems, that is the ideal. But life is not always ideal.

Chapter 3

Good Memories

There are always memories of some kind for all children and youth. Some may be good and have positive impacts in later life. So it was with Ronald. One of the biggest parades in Hawaii in the early 1950s was the Memorial Day Parade, aka Armed Forces Day Parade. It was held near the Ala Moana Park-Waikiki Beach area with the main marching taking place along Ala Moana Boulevard. Real United States Military personnel marched. Members of the University of Hawaii R.O.T.C. (Reserve Officers Training Corps) marched also. It was a requirement for all males to take R.O.T.C. as part of their education. One could choose either the Army or the Air Force R.O.T.C

Ronald attended one of these parades with his parents. He was awed by the marchers, and he enjoyed a picnic lunch at the Ala Moana Park. A few years later, he went to the Memorial Day Parade with some of his friends. They enjoyed the parade, but of even more excitement was exploring some of the World War II memorabilia present on the grounds of the Ala Moana Park. He will never forget getting close to the "Flying Tiger" fighter airplane, and the tanks on display! There were displays of combat gear as well.

The Waikiki Beach-Diamond Head area was not a really big tourist area when Ronald was growing up. One of the places he and his family liked to visit was the Honolulu Zoo located in Waikiki. On the park grounds were really large Banyan trees with vine-like appendages hanging down from the huge branches. As a child laying under those gigantic trees, he imagined being like Tarzan and swinging from limb to limb in a jungle with wild animals around him!

During the summer there were trips to the beach in Waikiki. Those were the days when the beach was clean and the water clear. Not a sign of pollution was found then. Once done, they would go and shower in the large bathroom/shower adjacent to a nearby pool where world-class swimmer Duke Kahanamoku practiced. None of them became world-class swimmers, but these trips made for positive memories.

Good Memories

It was the mother of one of Ronald's friends who made all of these trips possible for her two sons and their friends. This was what neighbors did for each other. This same mom also provided transportation for her sons, Tom and John, and for Ronald during their elementary and junior high school years.

In Hawaii, in the 1950s, it was considered a good thing if one was a Japanese-American. If you were from a well-to-do family, that was even better. But if you were a Filipino-American, you were looked down upon. Racial prejudice was not something that involved only blacks and whites. Bullying often took place between these different social groups.

For example, Don came from a good home. He was not a poor Japanese-American farm boy. He lived in the better part of Honolulu and played halfback on a football team. And he dressed well for a sixth grader at Waialae Elementary School. On the other hand, Paul was definitely not privileged like Don. He dressed like the poor children did. He was a Filipino-American. He may not have been a "good" Japanese-American boy, but he showed more sense and maturity than Don and Ronald did.

Don and Ronald were in the sixth grade

at the time. School had ended and the two friends were hanging out together when all of a sudden, as some girls approached, Don became belligerent. He began to shout at Ronald and get in his face, challenging him to a fight. Ronald was no match for Don. Ronald was skinny, slow, and clumsy.

Paul was nearby, lying on his back on the grass, minding his own business. But Paul quickly realized what was happening. He got up and ran over to where the commotion was and held Ronald back. Ronald became hysterical, yelling and sobbing, "Let me go, Paul. Let me go!"

But Paul held on to Ronald and calmly said, "No, Ronald, you'll get hurt." After a short while, Don left. By that time, the girls had passed on by.

Years later, Ronald still remembers the poor Filipino boy who was a godsend at a very critical moment in his life. Just having a better home, good clothing, and other advantages that money can buy does not necessarily mean that children will have good character. Paul proved that to Ronald that day.

During his elementary school years, Ronald read a variety of books as part of his class work. He discovered that he really enjoyed books, especially ones about the

American frontier. Through these books he became familiar with great men such as Davy Crockett, Daniel Boone, and Lewis and Clark, He loved reading novels about frontier adventurers. He also enjoyed reading novels involving baseball players.

After reading these books he wanted a BB gun so he could go hunting. When his father said no, Ronald decided he would make a slingshot using the branches of a neighbor's Oleander shrub, rubber bands, and some old leather he found. He first selected branches to form the "Y" shape he needed. Then he peeled the skin off and let it dry. He joined the rubber bands together, tied them to the arms of the slingshot on one end and attached the piece of leather for his "bullets" to the rubber bands. He practiced by shooting cans at a distance. When he became good enough, he went hunting in the bushes across the street from his home in Waialae. He shot doves and sparrows. The doves were big enough to sell to his uncle for a quarter. The sparrows were grilled for himself and his mom. He also caught birds in a homemade trap, which he sold or brought home to eat. Those were his "frontier days!"

Ronald's other interest was baseball. Although he never became a good baseball player himself, he loved the sport, and he enjoyed playing the game. He became a fan of the St. Louis Cardinals. His hero, Stan "the Man" Musial, is still a very well-respected baseball icon. When the Cardinals went on a Pacific-Asian goodwill baseball tour, Ronald managed to save enough money to watch them play the Asahi All-Stars at the Honolulu Stadium. Although Stan Musial did not hit a homerun that day, St Louis centerfielder Bobby Gene Smith did. Ronald was in the wrong section of the bleachers to have a chance at getting that ball. But attending the game was an event Ronald would always remember, and at least the Cardinals won.

In Honolulu, what we know today as junior high school or middle school, was called intermediate school. So Ronald attended Kaimuki Intermediate School. It was located about one to two miles away from Waialae Elementary School; thus, that much farther from home. As mentioned earlier, a kind and caring neighbor provided transportation for Ronald and her sons to and from school almost every day. As with many Japanese-Americans, she was from a devout Buddhist family.

During the seventh grade, Ronald became friends with Stanley. Stanley was

Good Memories

from a middle-class home who lived in Kaimuki, where many of the Japanese-Americans lived. Stanley and Ronald shared a love of rock 'n roll music, which was sweeping Honolulu rapidly among the teenagers of that time. Among the popular singers of that time were Elvis Presley, Pat Boone, Harry Belafonte, Richie Valens, Fats Domino, Doris Day, and Connie Francis. There were also very popular singing groups.

What separated the two boys was that Stanley could really dance and Ronald could not. So Stanley offered to teach Ronald to dance. The first lesson was at his home. They had a good time. The next lesson was at Ronald's home. They had a good time again.

Unfortunately, that was the last time they enjoyed each others company. Ronald's grandfather saw the two boys dancing and was livid! That night he expressed his disapproval in no uncertain terms. As the patriarch of the family, his words had a very strong influence. Summarizing his thoughts, dancing was for sissies, and he didn't want a sissy in his home.

This was devastating for Stanley and Ronald. Ronald was forced to no longer be friends with Stanley. Stanley's older sister came to Ronald to find out what had happened because a good friendship had stopped so suddenly. Especially in the worst of times, the best comes out of

> *Especially in the worst of times, the best comes out of those who really care.*

those who really care. Stanley's older sister showed a lot more maturity and caring for a ninth grader, than some adults do in trying to mend broken relationships. After she and Ronald talked, Stanley understood what had happened. A few years later they met while attending R.O.T.C. classes at the University of Hawaii. They were cordial and respectful to each other, but they did not renew their friendship.

After the "dancing incident," changes were made in Ronald's home. He was given more chores around the home and farm. And he was required to start weightlifting training under the tutelage of his Uncle Marvin, who was on the United States Olympic Weightlifting Team and competed in the 1948 and 1952 Olympic games in London, England, and Helsinki, Finland.

So it was that weightlifting became Ronald's new hobby.

The positive side to all of this was what happened to Ronald. He learned responsibility, having to manage his time between keeping up with his homework, completing his chores, weightlifting, and playing with his neighborhood friends. His sports skills also improved. He was asked to tryout for a Pop Warner football team by one of the players on the team who was impressed with Ronald's speed and toughness on the field. Ronald was also asked to tryout for the high school varsity football team by the head coach, who was also impressed with Ronald's speed and ability to catch the football any way the passer chose to throw the football to him. His father never allowed him to participate in competitive sports, but Ronald could accept that. Just being considered was an honor for him.

Chapter 4

Other Memories

Unless we live in a bubble, in an imaginary utopia, no one has a perfectly happy childhood full of only good memories. Even the best homes experience challenges and difficulties that they must overcome. Ronald's life was not filled with just good memories.

One weekend Ronald's father and some of his friends and business associates decided to play cards. The money flowed as they gambled and bet on their card games. And there were snacks and beer for the participants.

But Ronald's father did not do well that night—he was one of the losers. After Ronald went to bed, he heard a thud and his mom crying. He peeked through the door and saw his father with fists clenched, kicking his mom, who was begging for mercy. This happened twice in their home at Waialae and at least once in Waianae. Spousal abuse is not a new phenomenon and it plagues many homes, but for Ronald it was a very scary and unforgettable scene that engrained into his memory.

If something good came from this experience, it happened years later right before Ronald prepared to get married, Ronald's

---

Prayer works, even for those who may not have much experience with talking to God.

---

mother had a very rare mother-to-son talk. It was very brief, but she pleaded with Ronald, "Please do not treat Lily like Daddy has treated me." Ronald understood, and he promised to treat his soon-to-be wife well.

Ronald had a number of other not-so-positive memories at school. The following two incidents happened after classes were over on the public school grounds. While it is true that this is not the norm, there is a chance that this could happen to anyone, and parents and adults who work with children and youth must be aware of these things.

Jane was a very petite, blonde who spoke very clearly. Her close friend, Mary, was heavy and stout. They were from another largely populated homeroom, so Ronald never really knew them. In fact, he had never talked to them until one afternoon when his ride was late and his friends were absent from school.

At Kaimuki Intermediate School, there was a field where crops were grown. Some areas were quite overgrown with plant growth. Ronald was minding his own business when Jane and Mary showed up.

Jane spoke softly, but clearly, urging Ronald to come into the bushes with the two girls and mess around.

"No," Ronald said emphatically.

The two girls tried several more times to tempt Ronald before they left. But this was not the end of the incident. A few months later there was a commotion in the girls' locker room. Mary was yelling at the top of her voice about Jane getting pregnant in the locker room.

About a year later, while going to a football game at the Honolulu Stadium, Ronald saw Jane carrying a baby with a tall young man by her side. Ronald was thankful for God's guidance and help in making good decisions, because otherwise he could have been the father of that baby in Jane's hands.

The second incident occurred under similar circumstances. Ronald's friends were absent, and his neighbor was late in coming to pick Ronald up from school. Ronald was waiting for his ride to come when Jimmy came along. Jimmy was slick dresser and had the reputation for being a gambler. It was also said that he armed himself well, having a switchblade pocket knife. Jimmy came on to Ronald that day and tried to seduce him into messing around in the bathroom.

Ronald forcefully said, "No." But Jimmy was persistent. Of course, Ronald was just as adamant in pushing Jimmy away. Ronald prayed for an escape and at that moment his ride came. So Jimmy quickly left. Fortunately, Jimmy never approached Ronald again. Prayer works, even for those who may not have much experience with talking to God.

The saddest part of all this is that Ronald did not discuss these two incidents with anyone at home or in school.

Ronald experienced another disturbing incident in high school after becoming acquainted with Lois. She was very quiet, but intelligent. She was also very thin compared to her younger sister, who was much heavier than she was. Ronald considered dating her at one time, but he could not muster the courage to ask her out.

Then one weekend during the school year he found out through the news media that a high school student had jumped to her death from the historic Aloha Tower, a landmark in the state of Hawaii. Built in 1926 it was the tallest structure in Hawaii at that time. Like the Statue of Liberty, it also welcomed thousands of tourists and immigrants traveling by ship. For Ronald and his classmates, it became associated with the death of their classmate. Like Ronald, many found out on Monday morning that the student who had jumped to her death was Lois. Apparently, she was the victim of child abuse. This was a very tragic event in their school and community. Everyone wished that this story could have ended differently and that one promising life could have made a difference in this world.

Chapter 5
Life Changing Events

Choices young people make have life-long implications for good or evil. During his eighth grade year, Ronald made new friends. These friends continued to be his friends through ninth grade. One of his classmates, Daniel, made a very positive impression on Ronald. Daniel was a good student who was not easily ruffled. He was not loud or boisterous, and he was a really good athlete and a true gentleman. Best of all, he was a sincere Christian! Daniel was the one person in school who Ronald respected and wanted to be like. But Ronald knew that at that time he could not be a Christian until he left home.

During the last quarter of his ninth grade year, Ronald's family moved from Waialae to Waianae. So as not to disturb Ronald's final year, the family decided to have him stay with Uncle Marvin and Aunt Jean. The only drawback was that he had to ride the bus to get to school and return to his uncle's home. One of his classmates,

Ben, also rode the same bus. On the bus after school, Ben would light up a cigarette and share a few puffs with Ronald. Ben was an excellent baseball player, but as Ronald recalls, even at that young age, Ben seemed to be short of breath. When he completed the ninth grade year, Ronald immediately went to Waianae to live and work on the farm for the summer before attending Waianae High School. This was a positive move that got him away from Ben. It was then that Ronald made a decision not to smoke again, and he never did.

When his family moved to Waianae, the family farm had to be rebuilt. While the construction was going on, Ronald was visited by a Jehovah's Witnesses representative, which his father allowed. They studied outside on the front porch of the family's Quonset hut. In the late 1950s, it was not uncommon to see Quonset huts here and there in the Waianae area. They had been used in World War II. One of these huts became Ronald's new house. They were well-built and affordable for the poor. His house stood for more than forty years before it was demolished.

One day while his father was finishing the last chicken coop, he was visited by an older Caucasian man dressed

Life Changing Events

conservatively. The man had a slight limp, balding forehead, and was heavy set. He offered free Bible correspondence courses to Ronald's father. But instead of enrolling himself in any course, Ronald's father enrolled Ronald in the Voice of Prophecy Bible correspondence course. Since Ronald did not have all the time in the world, he chose to discontinue studying with the Jehovah's Witnesses and just do the correspondence course.

In 1959 in the public schools that Ronald attended, homerooms were based primarily on your academic standing. Therefore, in the tenth grade if one was rated highly, one would be in homeroom 10-1, and the lowest rated students would be placed in the highest number, such as homeroom 10-20. The high school Ronald attended had six homerooms, and he was assigned to homeroom 10-4. The high school Ronald was supposed to have attended had sixteen homerooms, and he was also assigned to homeroom 10-4.

Ronald made very good grades. He even had time to play football before classes began in the morning with other boys who were there early. He made some good friendships with his playmates. For some reason, Ronald was never promoted to a higher class level even though, when the teacher left for smoking breaks in the male teacher's lounge, Ronald completed his assignments first instead of goofing off like many of his classmates. It was only after his schoolwork was done that he would join the others in card games or gambling. He soon learned to stop gambling, because he used his lunch money to pay for his losses. Fortunately, playing cards usually did not involve money. So that was the choice of most of Ronald's friends in class.

The following year he was promoted to homeroom 11-3. Before the first quarter was over, his homeroom teacher decided that Ronald was not in the proper homeroom, so she placed him in homeroom 11-2. In the meantime, Ronald made more friends. All this may seem normal, but Ronald stuttered very severely.

As far back as the third grade, he had problems with stuttering. At the close of his junior year in high school, he decided to run for student body treasurer. His opponent was a well-established Waianae High School student. The day came for campaign speeches to be made in front of the whole student body. All the candidates gave their speeches except for Ronald. Instead, Ronald's campaign manager spoke

Life Changing Events

for him. But when the votes were counted, Ronald won by a landslide.

The faculty was stunned. So was his opponent. Ronald's upset win was not just by chance. He had become friends with

---

We may not know what is in store for us, but God knows.

---

as many students as he could. It did not matter to him whether they were wealthy or not, popular or unpopular, talented or not talented, highly intelligent or not. Of course, there were some who did not become his friends. He became friends just to be friends. They were his "brothers" and "sisters."

He became friends with athletes from the varsity and junior varsity teams; with Christians, Buddhists, and students from other faiths; and with Hawaiians, Japanese, Filipinos, Caucasians, and other kids of mixed racial backgrounds. He had the support of most of the school pep squad-cheerleaders and song leaders. Angela, one of the most popular girls in high school, a song leader and friend since the first time they met in the tenth grade, was his campaign manager. And while Ronald gave no stirring speeches, he talked to students one-on-one, asking those he knew for their vote and their support. It was enough to turn the tide in his favor. One of his friends told him, "Of course you will have my vote and support. I know you can be trusted with our money. You are the only person I have ever known who paid me my gambling winnings as soon as you said you would!"

His network of friends was there for him. And to this day, he remains the best of friends with some of those he met in high school. No one can see the future, only God. Opportunities in the present can be building blocks for the future. We may not know what is in store for us, but God knows.

One of the new friends he made while in homeroom 10-4 became an important influence in Ronald's life. She was an active Christian leader, and they attended the Inter-School Christian Fellowship Club together. During the club meetings they would pray, sing gospel hymns, and share their faith. These meetings helped Ronald nurture his growing interest and commitment to becoming a Christian.

After graduating from high school, Ronald enrolled in classes at the University

Life Changing Events

of Hawaii and got a job working for a faculty member as a live-in gardener. He had to work four hours each weekend, and in exchange he lived in a room attached to the garage. It was small, but it worked. He had a bathroom and a bedroom and a hot plate to cook on. His father brought him home cooked meals once a week, usually enough for two days without refrigeration. On Sundays he would go to one of his uncles and aunts' homes for dinner. Once or twice a week he and one or two of his friends from Waianae High School would have dinner at a restaurant in Moilili, almost two miles from where Ronald roomed. It made for a pleasant walk in the late afternoon.

Even though Ronald wanted to eventually become a minister/evangelist, he did not know where to go for guidance. It was no secret that he stuttered a lot. The head of the religion program at the University of Hawaii was an atheist. Yet he, in cooperation with the Speech Department, assisted Ronald in initiating sessions with a speech pathologist. Because of this, Ronald was also able to pass the speech class required of all freshmen.

Meanwhile, Ronald completed the last of the courses offered by the Voice of Prophecy Bible correspondence school and decided it was time for him to keep the biblical Sabbath. At that time (1963), Hawaii was organized as a mission and not a conference. Since Ronald did not know how to find a church, he looked in the telephone directory to locate the nearest Adventist Church. It was then that he found the address for the headquarters of the Hawaiian Mission of Seventh-day Adventists. He went there expecting to find a church but was greatly disappointed when he found an empty office building. This could have been the end, but it was not.

He decided to look around. Near the mission office was a home. Ronald knocked on the door. The family living there was preparing to leave for the Seventh-day Adventist Church located in Kaimuki. Ronald went with them to church. At the end of the service, the family gave him directions to the Honolulu Central Seventh-day Adventist Church, which was easier for Ronald to get to by bus.

The following Sabbath Ronald traveled by bus to the Honolulu Central Seventh-day Adventist Church. This time he had no problems finding the church. Pastor Matthew was even kind enough to arrange for transportation for him for several weeks after learning of Ronald's transportation

Life Changing Events

needs and his desire to keep the Sabbath.

After meeting with Ronald over the next few weeks, the pastor felt he should prepare for baptism. He then arranged for Ronald to attend the Japanese Seventh-day Adventist Church and study with the pastor of the Japanese Seventh-day Adventist Church, Pastor Thomas.

Ronald was baptized on May 25, 1963, by Pastor Thomas after attending the Honolulu Central Seventh-day Adventist Church and the Japanese Seventh-day Adventist Church for several months.

He made his decision with the knowledge and permission of his parents. Some family members expressed their concerns, mostly because of Sabbath-related employment issues. One of his uncles told Ronald of how difficult it was for families during the Great Depression. Ronald replied that he believed that God would take care of him and his family, if he ever had one in the future.

His baptism was the result of different factors that no one could have foreseen—the influence of good Christian friends in junior high school and high school and Bible correspondence school. When Ronald was baptized, he attempted to find out who that unknown person was who had given his father the correspondence course materials. When he described him to other members of the Seventh-day Adventist churches he visited on the island, no one had any recollection of a man like the one Ronald described. Although it is possible that this was an angel, this unknown man truly did the work of an angel. The Lord works in mysterious ways! This same Lord continues to work for our salvation now as He did so many years ago for Ronald!

One critical factor that must not be overlooked and forgotten is the membership of both congregations. Those who Ronald got to know were truly some of the nicest people one could imagine meeting. They nurtured him, accepting him for who he was, not who he should be. Even back then, potluck lunches were superb. There was always enough tasty food. Sometimes, Ronald was invited to the home of one of the members for lunch. At other times, there were activities that he was invited to. Like Ronald, we need to study to know about our faith, be nurtured by caring, sacrificing, well-grounded members, and in time, grow and mature.

After his baptism, Pastor Thomas and Ronald agreed that it would be best for Ronald to attend a Seventh-day Adventist college. Pastor Thomas suggested Union College in Lincoln, Nebraska. Ronald could work for most of his tuition, room, and board there. Pastor Thomas took the time to go to Ronald's home to explain to his parents about what Ronald was planning to do. After that Ronald applied and was accepted as a transfer student from the University of Hawaii to Union College. He had no money for an airplane ticket, but he had been awarded a scholarship to be used at the University of Hawaii. He appealed to the scholarship committee to be allowed to use the money for his airplane fare. For the first time, such a request was granted. The amount of the scholarship was exactly what was needed for the airplane fare! The Lord provided a way, as He will for us, even in the difficult times we live in.

Perhaps one of the toughest decisions Ronald had to make was to leave the family farm and pursue his college education. Before attending the University of Hawaii, his father offered Ronald the farm in sort of a partnership with his father. He did the same after Ronald completed his freshman year at the University of Hawaii. But Ronald truly believed that God had a place for him in His work, so he declined the offers.

However, his father was scheduled for minor surgery and requested that Ronald remain at home until he recovered. Ronald agreed. It would make things tight for Ronald. He would miss some of the introductory events for new students attending Union College, but he felt that it was necessary to help his father out. As things turned out, everything fell into place. The surgery went well, and Ronald did all the heavy work until his father was cleared for normal activities.

The time quickly came for Ronald to pack his bags and get ready to head to Nebraska. But before he left he had a going away party on the beach with some of his friends from high school. The sunset at the beach in Makaha was picture perfect. The party ended, and everyone had a good time. It was a very memorable occasion for Ronald.

Chapter 6

College Days

Ronald had no idea what was in store for him. It was the first time he had flown to the mainland. It would be very different coming from Hawaii to Lincoln, Nebraska.

While on the plane he had time to think of all the events that had led him from where he was to where he was going. He thought about the Bible correspondence courses, his baptism, Pastor Thomas advising him of his need to attend a Christian college, the strong support of his new church family, as well as support from his high school friends and his own family.

Ronald's itinerary was this: he flew from Honolulu, Hawaii on United Airlines to Los Angeles, California, and then on to Denver, Colorado. In Denver he transferred to Pioneer Airlines, which took him to Nebraska. When he landed in Nebraska (he can't remember if it was Omaha or Lincoln), someone drove him to the college campus.

Upon arriving on campus, he heard a familiar voice. "Oh, there's Ronald," piped

Rosie. Rosie was the only other student from the Honolulu Japanese Seventh-day Adventist Church in Hawaii who chose to attend Union College. She was with two other young ladies from Hawaii—Christy and Lily, whom she introduced to Ronald.

The four of them became instant friends. From that time on, they were inseparable. Lily was not always with them, but Rosie, Christy, and Ronald were constantly together, to the dismay of other students who wanted to date the young ladies from Hawaii. The other Asian young men started calling Ronald "powerful fellow." Ronald was naïve to some degree. Since he worked on the college construction crew, he actually thought they were referring to the heavy labor he did. In the course of time, someone set him straight. What people did not understand was that they were just the best of friends, enjoying a type of sibling closeness.

Five other young men from Hawaii attended Union College that year (1963)—four were freshmen and one was a sophomore/junior. Most of them needed to work to pay for their college tuition, supplies, and room and board. Some also had college education loans.

From the first day he arrived at Union College, Ronald made daily visits to the business manager or assistant business manager's office asking for employment. There was none. This went on for about four weeks. Mateo, Ronald's roommate, worked off campus. One weekend Mateo's partner-boss had to leave, so Mateo needed help. In the pinch, Mateo asked his brother Julio and Ronald to assist him. It was hard work cleaning the kitchen area of the Cornhusker Hotel in Lincoln, but the work had to get done. It was difficult trying to scrub stoves, grills, and the floor, which was covered with grease from all the meat that was served there. This was quite a contrast from cleaning the floor of the Union College cafeteria kitchen, which Ronald did several years later.

Not long after cleaning the hotel kitchen, he visited the business office again and was given a slip permitting him to start work as a construction laborer. He was ever so grateful. As he had been doing since he learned about tithing while living on the farm, Ronald made sure he paid his tithe. Ronald had tested God's promises regarding returning tithes to the Lord. While still in high school, he paid tithe on his allowance. He tithed his earnings as a farm laborer one summer, and he tithed any monetary gifts he received from well-wishers when he left Hawaii to attend Union College. He even tithed his earnings from working with Mateo that weekend at the Cornhusker Hotel.

Some may think that this was not a test of faith, but Ronald grew up in a non-Christian home. And he went to Union College because he was told that he could find employment on campus to help him cover his expenses there. For one night's work, there was not much tithe involved. But for someone who needs income to cover needs, tithe can be a lot of money. But Ronald was faithful to the Lord.

Years later after Ronald was married, he and his wife finally realized that they were returning the tithe to the Lord, not "paying" tithe. The Lord is faithful to His promises. Sometimes it may test our faith to return tithe to Him, but He is true to His Word, and He will provide for our needs when we return what is rightfully His.

Ronald loved working on the construction team. During the time he was at Union College, there were several projects in progress that he and his fellow student laborers were involved in. The addition of the new wing to Rees Hall, the women's dormitory, the construction of the industrial education building, and the building of the new high-rise men's dormitory were the major projects that were completed by the college construction crew. There were also renovations and/or additions to the library, broom factory, and science building.

One day while working on Rees Hall, the pouring of the concrete began later than usual. Because of this, darkness fell before the concrete work could be completed. Lights were put on the top of the hoist used to lift the giant wheelbarrows of concrete to the floor above that was being poured. One of the students went on the hoist to steady the two wheelbarrows. Tim, the assistant supervisor, operated the hoist. Orders were given to wait to get on the hoist until after it had stopped moving and was safe to board. Ronald was the next person to go with the load on the hoist. Tim ordered him to be sure the load was secure, but he told him not to ride with it and to stay away from the hoist. Seconds later Tim was blinded by the lights above, and he misjudged where to stop, causing the hoist to break. The load came crashing down with a large thud!

Fortunately, no one was hurt. Four or five of the crew members worked longer to clean up the mess and start repairs. They missed supper. They, including a very thankful

Ronald, were permitted to go off campus for a late dinner. Ronald believes that the Lord impressed Tim to not allow anyone to ride on the hoist just before the accident. It was

> *Through prayer, studying, and many short nights, Ronald did quite well in his classes.*

not the usual practice, but it was definitely what saved him from being hurt. If anyone had been injured that evening, the consequences would have been much worse than a damaged hoist that was repairable!

Several years later when construction on the new men's high-rise dormitory began, a scaffolding had to be made to accommodate the hoist that was to be used to lift materials for the building. Larry and Ronald were selected to put it together. They were the last of the original student crew who had worked on the women's dormitory. In retrospect, this was not a very safe job. They wore no safety belts, and the only safety equipment they had was a hard hat and a pair of gloves. Tim was there to

College Days

help supervise and secure the scaffolding as it went higher and higher. After it was completed, the men's dean's wife expressed her concerns about the safety of that undertaking. It was indeed a miracle that none of the students were hurt badly or died during the five years that the construction went on at Union College while Ronald was on the construction crew.

Tragically, one of the adult carpenters lost his life when he fell from the top floor of the new high-rise dormitory. Sadly, the men's dean's wife saw it happen. No matter who it is that dies, there is sorrow. The sorrow is sometimes greater when the community is small and close-knit, as was the case at Union College. The deceased carpenter had a son who was a student at Union College. The son was one of the students who worked on the crew that had worked on the women's dorm several years before. He was one of the nicest young men Ronald had the privilege of meeting and working with.

Ronald enjoyed his part-time job on the construction crew, and it helped to pay for his expenses. His job helped him to study, and study he did. Ronald studied hard to earn good grades. His goal was to become a minister, despite his stuttering. Through prayer, studying, and many short nights, Ronald did quite well in his classes. He also began speech therapy at the University of Nebraska, which had an excellent speech pathology program. His speech professor at Union College knew the director of the speech pathology program at the University of Nebraska, so he made the initial contact for Ronald. He greatly appreciated his professor going the extra mile to help him. It made a huge impact on his life.

Ronald never completely stopped stuttering, but he learned to communicate better. One of the greatest compliments Ronald received came from the head elder of the little church in Iowa that Ronald and a classmate served at as part of the ministerial training program for seniors. At the end of the year, he told Ronald that when the year began he thought it was a hopeless case, but that at year's end, he felt that there was hope for Ronald. He felt that Ronald could become a pastor.

During most of the 1960s through the early 1970s, there was much turmoil in our nation. On Friday, November 22, 1963, President John F. Kennedy was assassinated in Dallas, Texas. Ronald recalls the shock and disbelief that pervaded the campus as the truth of this occurrence sunk

College Days

in. It did not matter to most that he was a Catholic. It mattered that the president of the United States had been shot and killed. The assassination of Martin Luther King Jr. followed almost five years later when the great leader of the Civil Rights Movement was shot and killed in Memphis, Tennessee, on April 4, 1968. It was sad that this leader who had wanted to make a stand in a non-violent way became a victim of violence.

Protests were not uncommon. Colleges and universities were part of this unrest. The peaceful demonstrations for civil rights was one part of the picture. But this was not the only thing. The country was involved in the very unpopular Vietnam War. At that time, the selective service was an important part of the nation's military structure. All males were to register with the Selective Service when they turned 18 years old. They were then subject to be drafted into the United States military. The Vietnam War continued to escalate during this period of time. This meant more draftees were needed to fight the war. There were protests across the country against the United State's involvement in the war and against the draft. This was also the time when the "hippies" began to influence modern culture.

In spite of the turmoil around the country, there was a sense of security at the college. One of the many positive programs at Union College was the Host Family Program. Faculty and staff and members of the College View Seventh-day Adventist Church "adopted" students from overseas, including Hawaii, so that they would have a home away from home, since these students usually couldn't travel home for holidays or leaves. One of the faculty members did her best to assist the students from Hawaii as much as she could since she had previously taught at Hawaiian Mission Academy and considered these students as part of her extended family. The faculty, staff, and church members were truly a blessing to the "adopted" students.

During Ronald's junior and senior years, he became part of a group of students who reviewed materials just before a quiz or exam. The regular members of that group always made A's, to the dismay of others in the classes they took together. Sharing what they knew helped reinforce their knowledge of the subject matter while learning from each others' knowledge. Only four members of this group received "calls" from a local conference. This meant they would be sponsored and could attend the

College Days

seminary without having to work to pay for their expenses.

Ronald was not sure what he was going to do. One day he was called into the office of the head of the Religion Department. He was asked if he accepted the decisions of the General Conference of Seventh-day Adventists as the final authority regarding church matters. Ronald responded that his final authority was the Bible and the writings of Ellen G. White. This was the wrong answer for anyone who wanted to be a minister in the Seventh-day Adventist Church. Even though Ronald knew this would cost him and his wife dearly, he answered according to his conscience.

Up until that office visit, Ronald had been one of the senior readers for the Religion Department. He needed the work to supplement his income earned by working on the construction crew. After that visit he found that his work hours slowly dwindled and his services were not as welcome as they had been.

By that time he and Lily were married. She had plans to complete her degree in elementary education in the summer. However, they did not have any invitations for employment, except for consideration for employment in the state of Minnesota near the border of Canada. Since both of them were from Hawaii, they decided that it would be too cold for them, so they decided against that.

Ronald and Lily prayed for some positive employment opportunities. They were still committed to working for the Lord. One summer afternoon Ronald met the head of the Education Department in the hall of the administration building. The dean asked Ronald about his prospects for employment. Ronald told him that he had none. Shortly before Lily completed her degree, they both received calls to work in Glendale, California. Lily would be teaching at the Glendale Adventist Academy Elementary School, and Ronald would be working for the Voice of Prophecy Bible correspondence school. It was not until the heads of the Education Department and the History Department began to be involved in finding employment for both Lily and Ronald that things began to look better for the young couple. After waiting patiently, God opened up the right doors.

Chapter 7

Important Lessons From College

Prayer is an important part of our lives as Christians. Prayer helps, although not always in the way we may expect. It was with much prayer that Ronald was able to attend Union College. The application, transfer of credits, acceptance, and travel accommodations were done in rapid succession without the aid of today's rapid electronic communication systems.

When Ronald arrived at Union College, he had hoped to find employment right away. But after taking the matter to God in prayer, he finally found work on the college construction crew. This led him to work for Sam and Tim, two of the nicest people one could know. As long as they could, they kept Ronald employed during the five years it took him to earn his degree in religion. This allowed Ronald and his wife, Lily, to graduate from college debt free.

It is true that it cost less to attend private

colleges in the 1960s, but wages were also very low. Sometimes one must choose between taking longer to complete a college/university education with little or no debt or getting done faster with loans to pay.

When Ronald took some very challenging courses at the University of Hawaii and at Union College, he put forth his best effort, but he needed help. He prayed, and help came to him in different ways. Jeb, one of Ronald's classmates from high school, found out that Ronald had a D in

> *...our perception of things may not be how others may perceive them.*

English Composition for the first semester. With Jeb's tutoring and Ronald's perseverance and God's blessings, Ronald was able to bring his grade up to a B, resulting in his passing with the required C average for the year for that course.

Ronald also struggled with algebra. Dr. Smith was a brilliant person, but Ronald drowned in his class, and dropped the course with an F. Instead, he took a business math class and passed with a B.

Important Lessons From College

During the second semester, he took college algebra again. This time he did very well, He was one of the top students in his classroom. The professor, Miss Chan, presented the same material in a different manner. With God's help, personal effort, and a different professor, Ronald passed the class. Unless one is gifted, learning takes some personal effort.

Greek was another class that Ronald had to work hard at. He was required to take two years of Greek, and it was with much prayer, studying, and very little sleep that he was able to do better than he ever dreamed he would. While taking second year Greek, he became the reader for the third-year Greek class.

Prayer works. But because God hears and answers us according to His will, the result may not be what we may expect. But it may be the best thing for us in God's grand plans. Ronald needed to have passing grades to graduate from college. He also needed employment. By doing well in his classes, he was recognized by his professors, and he became a reader for the Religion Department for most of the five years he was at Union College.

All too often, our perception of things may not be how others may perceive them.

The original construction crew was made up of young men of different backgrounds, goals, and situations. Some lived off campus, most lived on campus. Some were married, most were single. Most had some idea of what major they wanted to pursue, a few were undecided. A few of them did not have very good reputations. Ronald did not know that two of the young men he worked with had reputations for being "wild." To him, they were coworkers and friends. They worked together and ate together, but they rarely socialized beyond their work environment.

Years later Ronald found out that some faculty members had been concerned for Ronald because he had been seen in the company with these two students in particular. Ronald was shocked because he never thought of these two students as being bad. Yes, he knew they enjoyed playing their electric guitars some nights. But some of Ronald's friends and neighbors in Waianae did the same thing.

One summer Ronald was approached by another student to be co-leader for the Summer Missionary Volunteer Sunshine Bands. He agreed. This student handled the up front stuff, while Ronald arranged for motivational speakers to speak on the

Important Lessons From College

fruits of the spirit. He also made sure signs were posted in visible areas to arouse curiosity. That summer had one of the best turnouts for Sunshine Bands on Sabbath afternoons. The missionary volunteer leader for the summer recognized this on the final meeting on a Friday night but did not give any credit to Ronald for his assistance. Even though Ronald did not get any recognition for his efforts, he realized that other students recognized his efforts.

During his years at Union College, Ronald often had to fight back against discouragement through much prayer. For instance, Ronald worked for Elder Wade and took a class from him. He respected the man, but when Elder Wade suggested that Ronald consider being a librarian at the seminary, Ronald had to politely disagree with his professor that this was not his calling. A Japanese-American minister tried to discourage him from pursuing the ministry as well. He tried to reason with Ronald regarding his speech problem even though he had made some progress. Ronald did not take the advice of these two good men. Despite this, the Lord worked in his behalf by opening other doors for him.

Just because one does well in class and gets good grades does not mean one will get the kind of employment one may be preparing for, nor does being active in positive extracurricular activities. One of those who did not receive a call to the ministry was also the senior class president. He also participated in worship services, played his violin for special music, and taught a very interesting Sabbath School class. Ronald served as the treasurer for the Ministerial Club. He also participated in off-campus activities at the University of Nebraska. We may think we have things under control, but God is the One in control of our present and eternal good.

Chapter 8

Places and Persons

The Voice of Prophecy was a major part of the Adventist Church's media ministry. It was founded by H. M. S. Richards Sr., a pioneer in religious radio broadcasting. The Bible correspondence school was an important part of that program. In 1967 a Union College graduate went to work for the Bible correspondence school, but she was unhappy and left.

That opened the door for Ronald to join the Voice of Prophecy staff. Almost from the start the supervisor and Ronald got along very well and became good friends. Ronald did what he could to make it easier for his coworkers, even if it meant taking care of the trash pick-up for each work station when janitorial services were limited. Despite all the positive things that made for a good work environment, there was one problem. Ronald was not earning a livable wage. The supervisor did what she could, but her hands were tied. Because Lily was married, she was also earning lower wages, even though it was more than Ronald's wages.

During their stay in Glendale, they were especially blessed by their Sabbath School teacher, who was an employee at the Southern California Conference of Seventh-day Adventists office. His thought-provoking questions and suggestions helped Ronald years later when he taught Sabbath School classes in other churches.

Moreover, the young couple learned a little bit about the difficulties and challenges of life. Lily's two sisters worked at the White Memorial Hospital and lived in Boyle Heights. Apparently, their expenses exceeded their income, and on Friday nights, they would show up, knowing that Lily would be preparing a meal for Sabbath. The first few times this happened, the meal for Sabbath was gone on Friday night. So Lily learned to prepare enough food for Friday dinner and Sabbath lunch. This continued for some time. It was a good experience for all involved. The three sisters look back on those Friday nights as a positive experience. Although it seemed impossible, the Lord stretched Ronald and Lily's means. Years later, the sisters helped Lily and Ronald when they encountered unexpected difficulties as well.

Places and Persons

During their second year in Glendale, Lily and Ronald decided to move. Lily received a call to teach at the Fir Grove Seventh-day Adventist School in Vancouver, Washington. Ronald would be working for United Medical Laboratories across the Columbia River in Portland, Oregon, as a trainee in cytology. His long-range goal was to become a registered cytotechnologist. In the summer of 1970, they moved to Washington. Although they could barely afford the move, they made it. As they traveled, they were able to enjoy the rich scenery of Northern California—the Redwood forests and beautiful shoreline—as well as the Southern Oregon coast.

When they arrived in Oregon, Jon and Carrisa, former classmates from Union College, helped Ronald and Lily get settled. They gave them some money to help them pay for the added expenses of settling in a new town. They said they knew what it was like to be in need of help and to have someone help them and not expect to be repaid. They just told them that when they could help someone else, to do so. Ronald and Lily never forgot this lesson of kindness.

Lily loved the new school. She got along well with her fellow staff members. The principal and his wife accepted Lily and

Ronald as their extended family. And more than forty years later, they are still the best of friends.

Ronald entered a new and very foreign field of employment. It was difficult for him, but with much studying, hard work, prayer, and God's blessing, he learned his job. It was challenging, but he enjoyed it. And he loved the people he worked with.

The blessings that came from this friendship went very deep.

One day while working in the cytology preparatory laboratory, he met Linda. As he was working at his seat, she quietly approached him from the back, grabbed his shoulder, and said, "The Claw has got you!" (The Claw was a popular wrestler in the Northwest in the early 1970s.)

Ronald was shocked, and he turned to see who it was. But Linda was already walking out of the room. The prep lab supervisor and others said to ignore her. "She does things like that! That's crazy Linda!"

Not too many days later, Linda asked Ronald for a favor. They did not live too far from each other, and she needed a ride

Places and Persons

to work. He said yes. Thus began another lasting friendship! Linda moved to another place that was closer to the school where her son, Joe, was attending. Come to find out, Ronald and Lily lived less than a block from the school. So Linda and Ronald carpooled together long before it was encouraged in places such as Los Angeles, California.

Linda would drop Joe off at Ronald and Lily's house, and Lily and Joe would walk to school at the correct time. After school, depending on what was going on in school, Lily and Joe would either wait at school until Linda came to pick Joe up or they would go to Ronald and Lily's and wait for Linda and Ronald to return from work. Sometimes, they would have dinner at Ronald and Lily's, and at other times, they would have dinner at Linda's.

The blessings that came from this friendship went very deep. Not only were carpooling and childcare needs taken care of, but Ronald and Lily were accepted by Linda's ex-in-laws as part of the family, which was beneficial their first Christmas in Vancouver. Lily was very lonely because Ronald had to work that day. Fortunately, Linda did not. Ronald and Lily were invited to Christmas dinner at Linda's ex-in-laws.

But Linda dropped by to see Lily before Ronald got home and before the dinner. She walked into the duplex and realized that Lily was not okay. Lily was crying, so Linda hugged her. "I should have known better. I should have come by sooner," Linda said.

Linda did more than save Christmas. She knew there was something lacking in Ronald and Lily's marriage. She nagged Ronald about taking Lily out more instead of staying home, especially after church on Sabbath. Little by little, Ronald tried to do what Linda suggested.

Ronald and Lily credit Linda with saving their marriage. The good Lord ultimately saves us and saves our relationships, but He uses different means to do this. Linda, who was a divorcee, knew what it was like to struggle, but she wanted the best for Ronald and Lily, so she helped them all that she could.

One of the difficulties of working for a medical-related institution is staffing on weekends. Except for Sabbaths (Saturdays), Ronald and Linda did not always have the same days off. On one of those days when Linda went to work and Ronald was off, Ronald and Lily decided to try something they had never done before. The smelt, a small silvery fish, were running, and they

Places and Persons

had heard that all you needed was a long-handled net, which you could rent from a fishing supply store, and some buckets to catch all the fish you wanted. So they embarked on an adventure. Joe went with them.

They stopped at the fishing supply store and rented a net. Then they found a spot that looked promising. They all took turns trying to catch the smelt. The smelt were there. One had to be blind not to see them. But no matter how hard they tried, they could not catch any of the fish. They watched as another fisherman came and filled his buckets up in a very short time. Before he left, he came by and tried to teach them how to do it. Most of the smelt they went home with that day were caught by the kind stranger. After the stranger left, they managed to catch one or two more before finally deciding that smelting was not for them. In retrospect, it was a miracle that none of them fell into the deep flowing river from the ledge where they were trying to net the smelt.

But there was an unexpected storm brewing. After completing an intense training program, Ronald became a cytology screener. A cytology screener evaluates pap smear slides primarily for early cervical cancer detection and other gynecological problems. Most of the screeners were trained in the same training program and were very good at what they did. But only a few of them were A.S.C.P. registered cytotechnologists. Because United Medical Laboratories engaged in interstate commerce (it was the largest interstate multi-service laboratory at that time), it had to meet higher standards for its professional staff. Some of the screeners were transferred to other departments. Ronald was transferred to the Toxicology Department, which was involved in drug screening for the United States Armed Services draftees.

With these changes Ronald and Lily had to make a decision as to what was the best choice for their future. Of course, they prayed about the matter. Then they decided that Ronald should apply to the School of Cytotechnology at the Los Angeles County-University of Southern California Medical Center in Los Angeles, California. Classes were to begin on February 1, but it was already January. Through the intervention of the director of the Cytology Department, Ronald was accepted into the program. Normally, they accepted only twelve applicants, but this time they accepted thirteen!

Places and Persons

When Ronald and Lily received word of Ronald's acceptance into the program, they saw God's hand guiding them, but they had to make another difficult decision. The weather did not look good over the next few days, but Ronald had to leave and head to Los Angeles in order to start class on time. Consequently, Ronald drove through one of the worst snowstorms to hit Northern California. He actually raced along with the storm, driving almost twelve hours in snow and sleet, trying to avoid the worst of it.

Ronald and Lily could not afford to maintain two homes. And with Ronald moving to Los Angeles, Lily received permission to leave her teaching position early. Ronald found a rental not far from where Lily had taught before in Glendale. When Lily came down from Washington, she inquired about employment in the area. She was about to accept a position at Glendale Adventist Hospital when Glendale Adventist Academy approached her with a temporary position. One of the teachers was going on family leave, and Lily would be filling in until the end of the school year. The next school year a position opened up at the White Memorial Adventist School, and Lily was hired for that position. This school was located about one mile from where Ronald was attending classes.

Ronald completed his program and took and passed the national examination for cytotechnology; thus he became an A.S.C.P. registered cytotechnologist.

Ronald and Lily wanted to move to a rural community. Ronald found a job with a pathologist in Coffeyville, Kansas. Things seemed fine until his employer lost a major account and could no longer afford to pay Ronald's salary.

Ronald and Lily prayed for guidance. Ronald telephoned his former school in Los Angeles. The school referred him to a laboratory in Merced, California, where one of Ronald's former mentors had moved to. After a few phone calls Ronald accepted a position in Merced.

During the time period when Ronald and Lily lived in Merced, they enjoyed some of the best years of their lives, and they made many lifelong friends in their community and church.

Lily taught school in the local Adventist school. And both of them were very involved in the local Adventist church. It was in Merced that the Lord blessed Ronald's ministry as a deacon, local church elder, and Sabbath School teacher. Lily was a great hostess, inviting strangers into their home on Sabbaths. She and Ronald also served as hosts to guest presenters who would speak to the church in Merced. They also opened their home for a branch Sabbath School sponsored by the Fresno Asian Seventh-day Adventist Church for members of the local Japanese-American community.

Lily and Ronald spent a lot of time visiting various members and their families. Sometimes one spouse was not a church member. But that did not matter to them; they still visited the family and became friends with both spouses. Two of these families had a number of girls in their home. Neither the church leadership nor the staff at school suspected anything, but many years later some of the girls spoke up about the physical abuse that had happened in their home.

After living in Merced for a number of years, Ronald and Lily moved to Medford, Oregon. It was there that Ronald applied some of his theological training to assist some of the members of the Medford Seventh-day Adventist Church. There was a very popular college professor who was attacking some core Seventh-day Adventist beliefs. So it was decided that seven lay members of the Medford Church work together to defend their beliefs by writing a pamphlet. Ronald assisted the group with his knowledge of biblical Greek.

Unfortunately, the person in question was the featured speaker for an upcoming camp meeting. The group of seven made sure they were in attendance. While the man spoke, Ronald feverishly took notes as the others listened to him. He was a mesmerizing speaker. When the speaker was done, the person in charge of the event stated that there was nothing wrong with what the speaker had said. He invited all present to stand in affirmation of the speaker and his message. Everyone except the seven who had developed the pamphlet in response to this speaker's claims stood. When Ronald went home, he studied his notes carefully, and he quickly discovered that the speaker had misapplied the Bible, using references to support his points that did not apply at all to the points he was trying to make! He shared this with others, and they agreed.

Soon after this incident Ronald began having health problems, so he and Lily decided to return to California. As they left the area, Ronald was hopeful that he had contributed to the work of the Lord and the

Places and Persons

preservation of His truths.

For the next several years, Ronald spent his time working in the plant nursery business. At first he was tasked with watering the plants, but he soon became a salesperson and then a purchaser. During this period, he was serving in his home church as a deacon and Sabbath School teacher for the young adult group. Like his class in Merced, it began small, but grew into a fairly good-sized class. This was because of God's blessing, personal effort on Ronald's part, and prayer. Ronald had learned from excellent teachers.

Then one day things changed again for Ronald and Lily. Ronald received a call to go to Peru to start a floriculture industry at Inca Union College. So he and Lily took some time off from their jobs and moved to Peru as missionaries.

Once in Peru, he and Lily began learning Castellano, which is a better form of Spanish according to his teachers. Ronald, with God's blessing, was able to grow bedding plants—pansies, baby's breath, and roses—which the college sold as cut flowers. Some of the people were impressed by what they saw.

Ronald and Lily made a number of new

friends in Peru. They got to know Jaime, the purchaser for the college, and Gabriel, the head of the music department, and his wife, Maria. Maria introduced Lily and Ronald to tasty Peruvian cooking. While Ronald worked for the college, Lily worked for the campus store.

The couple lived off campus in Chaclacayo. Lily really enjoyed shopping in the *mercado* (market) in Chaclacayo. The produce was very good. The *Mercado Central* (Central Market) in Lima was much larger, but it was also much farther away than one would want to drive several times a week for your fresh produce.

However, there was a problem with priorities regarding water usage. Ronald tried to resolve some of the unexpected problems, but to no avail. And in the end, Ronald's project lost out. After praying about the matter, they decided to return home to the United States where Ronald could pick up his previous job at the retail nursery he had worked for before leaving for Peru.

Chapter 9
Calm and Turmoil

In 1983 Ronald and Lily returned to the United States with very mixed feelings. They returned to the homeland in a time of economic recession. Fortunately, the nursery he worked at prior to leaving for the mission field accepted him back, which he was very grateful for. But with the economy struggling, it was a very difficult time for the nursery as well, and Ronald knew he needed to prepare for the future. Some suggested that Ronald become a grower and sell plants wholesale. Others suggested that he become a gardener.

But after thinking things over and praying about the matter, he decided to return to the laboratory. He went to talk to his former teacher at the medical center where he had attended classes many years before. Unfortunately, Audrey had bad news. The field had changed. So had the requirements for registry and maintaining one's registry/licensure. But she had an alternative suggestion, and she told Ronald to talk to another former teacher named Monica who had started another program in cytogenetic technology at the Los Angeles County-University of Southern California Medical Center.

After speaking with Monica, Ronald was accepted into the program. She usually took no more than four students per year, but she accepted Ronald as the fifth student in her program. Ironically, by the time the year was over, only three students finished the course—Ronald was one of them. Then they all passed the national examination and were certified. This was a challenging course for Ronald. It was with much prayer, long hours of studying, and persistence that enabled him to pass the course and take and pass the examination for national certification as well.

It is interesting to note that at the time when Ronald applied for the programs in cytotechnology (1972) and cytogenetic technology (1987), one was not required to have a bachelor's degree in biology, chemistry, or another related science. So long as one had a college degree in any field, one could apply for these programs. The prerequisites for these programs became much more stringent years after he had worked for several years in these fields.

Calm and Turmoil

Were these occurrences just coincidences, or was God's unseen hand involved in such matters?

Meanwhile, Lily returned to teaching. She filled in for a teacher who was on leave. Then she accepted a job at the White Memorial Seventh-day Adventist School, which was near the medical center that Ronald was taking classes at. This again made it convenient for both of them. Although located in Boyle Heights, an unsafe area of Los Angeles in those days, it was a good school with a very dedicated Christian staff. When Ronald had to drop Lily off at the school before daylight, Denny, the school maintenance worker, would be there. When Denny retired, Lily and Ronald found out that he had arrived early all those years to be sure Lily would be safe!

With their work situations taken care of, Ronald and Lily settled into church life at an Adventist Church not far from their home. In fact, they were asked to lead and teach the junior high school age group, and they were just getting to the point where they thought they were accepted by the class when the pastor told them that their services were no longer needed. However, they were asked to teach the next younger group since the couple who was teaching that group would be taking over for them.

Two weeks later, after they were no longer teaching the junior high school class, they were standing outside the church between Sabbath School and the worship service when two of their former students came over and asked them, "Why did you dump us?" What should they say to the two honest young persons wanting an honest answer? It was difficult to give an honest answer because they didn't want to make waves. All they could say was that the pastor told them they were no longer needed to teach that class. It was heart-wrenching for them.

Later they discovered that a wealthy member told the pastor that if his daughter and son-in-law did not replace Ronald and Lily in the class they were teaching, they were going to leave and go to another church. (Sad to say, the family eventually left that church.)

Ronald and Lily realized that churches are made up of people, and people are not perfect. Only God is. But they decided it was best to transfer their membership to another church in the area.

Upon receiving his certification, Ronald accepted a job at the University of California-Irvine Medical Center cytogenetics laboratory in Orange, California. Unfortunately, he encountered some difficulties there with his supervisor.

Meanwhile, Lily and Ronald were having difficulties in their relationship. They were both in counseling. It was a double whammy for Ronald. Trying to please a supervisor who made it very obvious who she favored and who she did not made the long drive to work harder. Difficulties at home made it even harder. But the Lord Jesus sustained Ronald and Lily, and they survived their personal crisis.

Ronald's difficulties at work took time to resolve, but things eventually got better. In answer to his prayers, the Lord provided at least one person, and possibly as many as three or four people, to be advocates for Ronald. When some of the people were transferred to another laboratory as "leased" employees, Ronald went with them and was not terminated. Not long after that, the difficult supervisor chose to retire early. Ronald's new supervisor treated him with respect and fairness. Ronald spent more than twenty years with the same technologists who he had begun with after passing the National Certification Agency exam for cytogenetic technologists. Ronald and his three other coworkers who worked together at the first laboratory where Ronald began his new career survived two takeovers by other laboratories. During the third takeover, Ronald chose to accept severance and not work. The Lord does not fail us. He cares about us.

While trying to survive a crisis in their marriage, Mike, an old friend and former

> *Fortunately, God looks at the big picture, and His forgiveness is free and available to those who ask.*

classmate, wrote to Ronald. He wanted to visit and catch up with Ronald, but Ronald was in a quandary. He did not want to say anything to Mike about the personal problems he and his wife were having. When he asked Lily what to do, she said she did not care. At a loss for what to do, Ronald chose not to respond at all—he was embarrassed. Many years later, he wrote to Mike and explained to him why he had not responded to the letter and asked for his forgiveness. Unfortunately, Mike never responded. Sometimes, when we try to resolve one problem in life, we end up with another problem.

Fortunately, God looks at the big picture, and His forgiveness is free and available to those who ask. And although Ronald and Mike have not patched things up yet, Ronald and Lily's marriage is still in tact by God's grace and God's grace alone.

In the midst of all this personal turmoil, Lily wanted to quit teaching. It was not just the difficulties in trying to resolve and save their marriage that brought this about, but it was also a very ungrateful person who called on Lily several times to bail her out of situations that she could not handle by herself that caused Lily to want to leave teaching and leave denominational employment as well.

But an assistant school superintendent suggested otherwise. She told Lily this was not a good way to leave denominational employment, leaving with a bad taste in her mouth. She asked her to give it another chance and teach at one of the best schools in the Southern California Conference. After praying and reconsidering the matter, Lily decided to accept the position. Amazingly, she loved it and retired from that school after teaching for more than twenty years there.

While experiencing turmoil in our lives, God can provide for us a calm that will steady our rocky times if we let Him.

Chapter 10
Addicted

While it is true that this chapter could be a part of the previous chapter, the scope of this problem in Ronald's life warrants a closer look. Some may not consider this a serious problem, but this addiction impacted his life for years.

Choices we make today affect us not only in the present but also in the future. What may seem innocuous at first can end up being poisonous and deadly in the end. To the novice hiker a forested area of poison ivy may appear to be just another nice, green undergrowth. Similarly Adam and Eve made a bad choice, even though they were informed in advance of the danger. Sometimes addictions may begin early in life, sometimes later. Most of the time, we make choices that determine what we are addicted to.

Ronald was not a saint. He had personal struggles to deal with, as all of us do, even after he was baptized. But one of these struggles became a real problem.

Soon after returning from Peru, he was given a California Super Lotto ticket for his birthday. Since it was a gift, he played, although he did not win anything.

The only links he had to gambling were from his childhood and youth, and the memories were not pleasant. His in-laws and stepfather went to Las Vegas to gamble. But he never went. He could not be enticed into going; he was not drawn to gambling in any form.

Unfortunately, conditions were different after returning home from Peru. He and Lily struggled to get back on their feet financially. They were sharing a rental house with Lily's sister who had just recently filed for divorce. Lily's sister was not doing well either. The economic picture for many was not promising in the 1980s. The nursery where Ronald worked at was not doing very well, which is why he eventually had to leave something he loved.

After that first free lotto ticket, he slowly began to play super lotto, but not on a regular basis. He could justify the occasional lotto purchase. First, he reasoned that it was to help the state of California's education system. Then, if he won, the Lord's work would be blessed from the tithe and offerings Ronald would give to His work.

Besides, if other people could win, why not he and his wife? They had nobler intentions to use the money for the Lord and to ease their financial struggles. Self-justification is easy.

Then came the ugly part. Unbeknownst to Ronald, certain persons made a bet to see if Ronald could be tempted to gamble in Las Vegas or not. Ronald and Lily were to go as guests of one of the bettors. The room accommodations and food was very affordable. While there the bettor taught them how to play the slot machines. Although the slot machines were not very generous that weekend, Ronald enjoyed himself. That was the beginning.

For more than twenty years, Ronald and Lily drove to Las Vegas whenever they had a break or vacation so that Ronald could gamble. Sometimes they would go once or twice a year, but more often than not they went about three to four times a year. When Las Vegas became a little bit pricier, Ronald and Lily began to go to Laughlin, Nevada, to gamble. But the preferred place was Las Vegas.

There were some positive things about all those years. During the first ten years or so, the trips were affordable, and it gave Lily a break from her busy days. While

Ronald gambled, Lily would sleep in and eat well. They also met a fine couple who became their friends. Tony was a bellman and Bobbie taught in a private Christian school, so they had some things in common. Bobbie and Lily spent a lot of time talking and sharing the joys and struggles of life. Ronald and Lily were also able to tour the area and see some of the natural beauty in the surrounding states. They enjoyed trips to Bryce Canyon and Zion National Park in Utah, the Grand Canyon National Park in Arizona, and Death Valley in California. They also went to Mount Charleston and Red Rock Canyon in Nevada before any casinos were built in that area.

During those years, Ronald never held any church office. He did not believe it was proper for him to do so. When asked he spoke to junior-earliteen Sabbath School classes as a presenter on special topics at other churches, but he wasn't asked to hold any office at his church, and he did not pursue doing so. However, he thoroughly enjoyed the opportunities he had to interact with church kids.

To help pay for their gambling trips, Ronald worked many overtime hours, including weekends. He also worked part-time as a salesperson for a local plant nursery on Sundays. They called him "Sunday Ronald." Some gamblers win enough during their weekend gambling trips to pay for the whole trip, including any money lost. Ronald *never* did that once in the twenty years he gambled. He had to

God's grace is available for everyone.

pay for his room, meals, car rental, and gambling money.

Somewhere, sometime, Ronald stopped and realized what he was doing. He was not as destitute as the prodigal son, but he needed to change. He began to listen to the voice of the Holy Spirit and his guardian angel, and he slowly began to realize that gambling was not an innocent entertainment experience. He would never be able to retrieve the money spent on the trips he and Lily had taken over the years. The time lost could never be regained. And although Ronald *never* gambled during the Sabbath hours, he knew he was not living the lifestyle he should.

There are at least two very important lessons to be learned from Ronald's addiction to gambling. First, one must never think that he or she is so good and strong to never fall to a particular temptation others enjoy. It is easy to fall. Once trapped it may be very difficult to escape.

The most important thing to remember is that the Lord gave Ronald time to come to his senses. In this respect, the Lord is truly merciful, not wanting anyone to be lost. He not only provided for Ronald and Lily's temporal needs, but he gave them time so that Ronald could, like the prodigal son, come to his senses and return to his Father's house. The process is not completed. There are other temptations that test Ronald, but God's grace is sufficient.

God's grace is available for everyone. Each of us are tempted in some way. If we fail, we have an Advocate, the Lord Jesus. His precious blood is the only argument we will ever need. But time is very short, perhaps much shorter than we may think.

The author hopes that those who read Ronald's story will find hope and learn to trust in the Savior, who died for everyone. Even in our darkest hour, Jesus is there. Whether you are like Ronald's mother, a single parent without a good source of income to support her family; a college student having to work to earn a degree, someone faced with a career change, or someone caught in the hold of an addiction, there is hope and forgiveness.

As the world nears the end, each of us must make a decision as to whose side we are on—God or Satan's. If you choose God's side, someday soon you will join the redeemed from all ages in heaven where we will worship the Creator and Redeemer forever, enjoying the river of life described by John in the last chapter of the book of Revelation.

The majority of this book has been devoted to Ronald's life story and the ups and downs he has experienced along the way in his walk with the Lord. The last few chapters of this book are experiences and insights Ronald has had over the years in regards to the Christian faith that he wanted the author to share with readers.

Chapter 11

Angels

Years ago Ronald met a psychiatrist who was bent on making Christians into unbelievers, and he was successful to some degree. He attempted to persuade Ronald by using this argument, "You believe in God. You believe in the Bible as God's Word. You believe in the existence of angels. But how can you believe all that if you have never seen an angel in a long white robe with shining long hair and two wings?"

Ronald tried to explain to him that angels do not always appear in that manner, but the psychiatrist was adamant in his stance. He allowed Ronald no time to present any other argument. Therefore, his conclusion was that angels do not exist, nor does God or His Word! If he would have listened, Ronald would have shared with him true experiences of divine intervention by angels. He would have told him the story of the snowstorm that Lily found herself in while attending college in the Midwest.

Angels

If you have ever experienced a blinding snowstorm, you know how easy it is to lose your sense of direction. Well, Lily was caught in a very heavy, blinding snowstorm on the college campus she was attending in the Midwest. Her class had finished so she began walking to her off-campus apartment, which was less then a mile away. Unfortunately, she could not see anything, and she did not know where she was or which way her home was. To make matters worse, she could not find her way back to the buildings on campus.

So she prayed for help. And believe it or not help came in the form of a St. Bernard, just like the large rescue dogs used in the Alps. The dog seemed to know where he was going, so she followed it. And the dog led her to her home. When she burst through the door into her apartment, Lily couldn't wait to recount the story to Ronald. They were both very thankful that the Lord had answered her prayer.

Several years later Lily was walking from the school she was teaching at to hear Ronald's presentation of his research project at the Los Angeles County-University of Southern California Medical Center School of Cytotechnology. It was a thirty-minute walk, but Lily did not mind. As she began her walk a large German Shepherd dog appeared and began walking in front of her. Surprisingly, the dog would stop at intervals and look back at her as though she were its master. After she reached her

---

The Lord is merciful and loving, not willing that any of us should be harmed or lost.

---

destination, the dog disappeared. Ronald was very relieved to see her. Anyone familiar with that part of Los Angeles, especially during that time, knew that it was very unsafe, even for locals. When they talked about her walk, she told him that there were some men eyeing her, but no one attempted to do anything because of the German Shepherd's presence.

Ronald and Lily felt that this was not a mere coincidence. God had heard their prayers for protection as they committed themselves into His care. Unseen angels may have guided the dog. Or an angel in the form of a dog led the way! The full story will not be revealed until they reach heaven.

While in Peru, Ronald experienced his

own dog story, but this dog had a nasty temperament. It was a black dog, and it belonged to one of the non-teaching personnel on campus. Unfortunately, it attacked a graduate student. The unprovoked incident made many people afraid of the animal.

Ronald was working to develop a new industry on campus, and he had a makeshift office on campus. One morning Ronald was standing outside his office facing the main road on campus. It was then that he saw the black dog with two of the school groundskeepers on the road walking in his direction. All of a sudden the dog charged at him full speed and jumped as if aiming for his neck. In the split second after the dog jumped, Ronald saw a bright flash of light appear between the dog and himself! Then the dog bounced backward and fell on the ground with a look of obvious fear and surprise on its face! The dog never bothered Ronald again. The construction workers made light of what happened, but Ronald knew that God had sent an angel to protect him from being hurt!

The Lord is truly merciful and loving, not willing that any of us should be harmed or lost.

Chapter 12
Other Encounters

Whether we are raised in a Christian environment or not, Satan and his angels do whatever it takes to prevent people from living for Christ here on earth and into eternity. These evil angels try to separate us from our Creator and Redeemer any way they can. The way Satan succeeded in tempting Adam and Eve to fall in a perfect environment, thus resulting in them losing out on Eden should tell us something about the wily foe we face. Satan also tried to tempt Jesus as recorded in Matthew 4 and Luke 4. Then men, inspired by Satan, crucified Jesus on the cross. These examples should tell us of the extent to which Satan will go to destroy us. Fortunately, there are holy angels who minister to those who ask for God's protection and help. Psalm 34:7 and Hebrews 1:7, 13, and 14 give us insight into this unseen world.

While in college studying for the ministry, Ronald asked Lily to marry him. It was during this time that she told him of some shocking experiences that had occurred while she was growing up in Hawaii, but also as a student at the college they were attending. While in bed, a force would overpower her, rendering her unable to move, say anything, scream, or breathe. Fortunately, this being was not permitted to complete its work. She lived to share her story. The attacks became more frequent after she was baptized and became a member of the Seventh-day Adventist Church.

Nobility and valor are admirable virtues. But sometimes we don't know what we are getting ourselves into as we try to save someone else. One night Ronald asked the Lord to let the unknown attacker attack him, rather than his fiancé. And that very night it did! As he slept, it overpowered him. Ronald could not move even though he struggled with all his strength. Ronald could not breathe. In utter desperation he said a silent prayer to the Lord. When he did that, three things happened almost simultaneously. A peaceful calm came over him, a light surrounded him, and he saw a grayish cloud-like form leave the room out of the window. This happened to him at least one more time. Worse yet, his fiancé continued to be attacked in the same manner.

What could they do to resolve this? They had no power to prevent these recurring attacks. They decided to seek counsel from one of the professors in the Department of Religion. He was a highly respected man on campus, and Ronald and his son were good friends. They related to him what had

---

This world of sin is full of challenges and difficulties.

---

happened in the past and was still happening to both of them. He told them that he had never experienced such attacks, but he knew another minister who had been confronted with similar attacks. He emphasized that only the name of Jesus could send these beings away. He had prayer with them. After that the attacks became few and far between. Ronald and Lily were grateful for this man of God who was willing to listen and pray with them about this personal matter of such importance.

Several years later during an ABC's of Prayer seminar, one of the presenters told of a similar experience. He was a big man, but he recounted how he was overpowered by a force that held him down. He was

Other Encounters

helpless and unable to move or breathe. He realized that this was no human being whom he was struggling with. He immediately repeated Psalm 23, verse 1—The Lord is my Shepherd...—as a prayer and continued to do so until the mysterious, powerful being left him!

We sometimes cannot explain everything that happens in life. Why are some people apparently never hurt or victimized in any way? Why are others victimized? Ronald does not have an answer, but he can speak to his own personal experiences. In addition to being saved by angels, over the years he and Lily have experienced heartache, pain, and suffering. This world of sin is full of challenges and difficulties.

On two occasions he and Lily have had their residence broken into. The first time there were some valuables stolen. The second time there was not much stolen. But both times no one was home and thankfully no one was hurt. Things can always be replaced. Our lives are much more precious than material things.

In addition, Ronald was also a victim of a mugging. He went to the laundromat early one Sunday morning, intending to go to work at his part-time job at a local plant nursery after getting the laundry done. As he drove into the parking lot, he noticed that something was not right. Usually, there were several other people there waiting to get in early. This time he was the only one there. So he went in and started the laundry. No sooner had he done that when four young Hispanic men came in. They smelled like they had been drinking, and they asked Ronald to buy them some liquor from the Seven-Eleven store adjacent to the laundromat. They said they had forgotten their IDs. Ronald politely said no, and that's when it turned violent.

One acted as a lookout while the other three made sure Ronald could not get away. One of them grazed him with his fist. Ronald knew he was no match for all of them, so he fell to the floor thinking they would relent. But they did not. They tried to stomp on him as he lay on the floor. Fortunately, they missed his head and neck, but they did get him in the rib cage and legs.

When Ronald realized he was in trouble, he called out to God, and almost instantaneously, he felt a calm come over him. Then the lookout shouted something, and they left in a hurry. Minutes later a man entered and helped Ronald call the police. After finishing the laundry, Ronald went home, and he and Lily drove to the emergency room so that Ronald's injuries could be looked at. After examining him, the doctor determined that Ronald had some bruised ribs, but no fractures. Ronald felt fortunate that he was not seriously injured or killed in the incident. And he thanked God for sending a good Samaritan to his rescue. The man told Ronald that he was impressed to go to the laundromat because he felt something was not right.

Chapter 13
Not Just Incidents

Ronald and Lily were occasional attendees to a Friday evening worship group that met at the school where Lily taught. The principal usually led out in the meetings, and one time he shared the story of an incident that occurred when he and his family traveled to the beach before the start of a new school year. He was at the wheel, his wife was in the front passenger seat, and his two daughters were in the backseat. He related that all of a sudden an object appeared on the freeway in front of him, and he had no choice but to hit the object. This, of course, sent the car airborne! As the car flew above the center divider, he wondered if this was how it was to end for them. But the car miraculously landed on the other side of the highway, and the whole family walked away from the accident with very little injuries to speak of. Furthermore, he had his mechanic look at the car, and the car was not damaged as badly as one would expect. After hearing this, one of the teachers said, "The Lord has a work for you to do here!"

This reminded Ronald of another incident. Lily's sister had a condominium in Palm Springs, California. The main route from Los Angeles to Palm Springs is Interstate 10. Ontario International Airport is located just west of where Interstate 10 and Interstate 15 intersect. Family members would sometimes vacation in Palm Springs and stay at the condominium.

On one of these occasions, Lily's sister-in-law and two nieces came to Palm Springs to visit Lily's mother, who spent much of her vacation in Palm Springs,

"The Lord has a work for you to do here!"

away from her home in Hawaii. Ronald and Lily were there, too, because they had keys to the place and were available to help with transportation. The night before everyone had to leave Palm Springs was wonderful. Everyone had a good time and went to bed late.

When it was time to leave on Sunday morning, everyone was running a little late. So they skipped having a group prayer as they normally did before traveling. They piled the luggage in Ronald's car, and the rest of the group got into Lily's car. Then Ronald led the way from Palm Springs to the Ontario International Airport. They were making good time, and traffic was moving at a steady rate, but trouble was up ahead. When they were about three or four miles from the intersection of Interstates 10 and 15, Ronald prepared to change lanes so that they could continue westbound on Interstate 10.

He checked his mirrors and saw a white car in the lane some distance behind them, so Ronald changed lanes, as did Lily. But when Ronald glanced in his mirror again, to his amazement, he saw the white car speed up. It was on a collision course with Lily's car, and Ronald couldn't do anything but watch helplessly in his rearview mirror. Lily tried to avoid a collision, but the white car hit the left rear wheel of her vehicle, which damaged the rear brake system. Lily tried to stop the car, but nothing happened when she hit the brakes. She crisscrossed the westbound interstate four times, avoiding crashing into a fence on the right side of the interstate, before coming to a crashing halt at the center divider.

While she was crisscrossing, Ronald could only watch in horror and pray. But something strange happened. Only the white car drove by. There was plenty of traffic behind Lily's car, but it seemed as though there was an invisible wall separating her car from all the other cars. When she came to a stop, a witness stopped behind her and stayed as a witness to tell the California Highway Patrol officer that it was a hit-and-run accident. The officer told Lily that she was very fortunate and that Someone must be watching over her. The officer then told Lily that just the night before a fellow officer had been killed crisscrossing lanes on the freeway.

All things considered, God protected them during this accident. Lily's sister-in-law and two nieces made it to the airport in Ronald's car while an ambulance took Lily's mother to a nearby hospital for treatment of a few injuries because of the crash.

One thing was a mystery to Ronald and Lily. They drove by the location of the accident several times looking for the fence on the right side of the interstate, but there was no fence in that location.

Ronald experienced God's protection in another driving incident, but this one happened on a trip from Jackson, Tennessee, to Nashville, Tennessee. Ronald and Lily were unfamiliar with the highway or the weather in Tennessee during the summer. All of a sudden, they found themselves driving in a blinding rainstorm, and they could not see anything. They drove slowly and prayed, but it was very scary. They safely made it through the storm thanks to God's protection.

On another occasion, Ronald was on his way home from work when he was cut off by red Ford Mustang driven by a young lady. She was obviously in a rush. Traffic had slowed down almost to a stop, so Ronald changed lanes and passed the Mustang. The young lady changed lanes and followed Ronald as they both made the transition to the westbound 10. Ronald wasn't sure what was going through the driver's mind, but she tailgated him until they were on the westbound 10. Then she changed lanes, passed Ronald, and tried to get in front of him. But she could not. Some unseen force kept her from doing so. Ronald watched tensely as she looked as if she was about to cut him off again, only to see her be held back and not able to complete the lane change. Ronald could see the frustration on her face. After several attempts, she sped away and drove out of sight.

These incidents are all true occurrences. Nothing is fabricated. Ronald believes that these stories are examples of how God takes care of His children. Even though we are undeserving of His love, God is with us, and His angels are there to intervene on our behalf, seen or unseen.

Chapter 14

Binding

Looking back on Ronald's life, some may wonder as to why he remained a Christian after some negative and devastating life experiences. When the head of the Religion Department treated him differently and encouraged him *not* to go to the seminary because he chose the Bible and the Spirit of Prophecy as his final authority, Ronald still remained faithful to God.

He also continued following God after his missionary term to Peru came to an abrupt halt. He had gone there with hopes of serving God and helping to establish a profitable enterprise for the school. On his way to Peru, Ronald had stopped in Miami and visited with a major supplier in the floriculture industry. The man said he would have a market for Ronald's enterprise if he would grow a certain plant for seeds only.

But upon arriving at the school, Ronald was told by the administrator that he was sent to grow flowers, not green plants. When the Lord blessed his efforts with flowers, there was a conflict with another college industry over using water from the well. Ronald was told to use "agricultural" river water instead. In an attempt to resolve this problem, Ronald and another professor tried to gain approval from the administration to get windmills set up on campus to pump water from the water table below. This would also have produced electricity for use on the campus. But the

---

God alone is the one who sustains us....

---

proposal was refused. Greatly disappointed, Lily and Ronald decided to return home earlier than they had planned.

Ronald was told by some that they respected him for the decisions he made in both of these life-changing situations. But respect does not quite make up for the resulting personal devastation these decisions brought on Ronald and Lily. Some people have gone one step further and asked why they still attend church. The answer is that no one is perfect. Everyone makes mistakes. God alone is the one who sustains us in poverty and prosperity, in sickness and in good health, in disappointment and in success. Even though some may not respond as we may think they should, we still need to remember that we worship a God who cares about us.

And then there are times when we need to make choices because of circumstances we have no control over. In 2003 the state of California initiated changes for people employed as cytogenetic technologists. Up until then workers in this field had to pass a national examination and be nationally certified to be employed in a state licensed laboratory. But things changed. The new regulations said that, in addition to national certification, cytogenetic technologists in California had to have either a bachelor of science degree in biology, chemistry, cytogenetics, or a bachelor of arts degree with twenty-five semester hours of biology and/or chemistry. Ronald had only six semester hours of biology.

Ronald and Lily prayed about the situation. They also attempted different solutions. Ronald spoke to the person in charge of the licensing procedures several times. He also tried to have the state count his year of attendance in the School of Cytotechnology, since the curriculum was very heavy on biology. Furthermore, attempts were being made to have a

"Grandfather clause" added to the licensure bill, but to no avail. It became obvious that Ronald would have to decide whether to go back to school or leave and find another field of employment.

Unexpectedly, his supervisor called him into his office and told him, "Ronald, you are going back to school." The company agreed to pay for the expenses of obtaining nineteen semester hours while Ronald worked part time. The goal was to complete nineteen semester hours in one year's time. That sounded simple until Ronald tried to enroll in classes for the fall semester. Most of the colleges and universities had waiting lists for the classes he needed.

In the meantime, Ronald and Lily continued to pray. Then the answer came. As he considered a solution to his predicament, he contacted the director of the Biotechnology Program at Pasadena City College. Dr. J invited Ronald to an interview. She was very understanding of his situation, and she told him to go ahead and enter the classes he needed for the fall, winter, and spring terms. She then let her colleagues know that Ronald was coming to class. So it was that the Lord helped Lily and Ronald survive a personal crisis. And he received his license in June 2004. It was not easy, but with the Lord's blessing, the support of his wife, friends, and colleagues, another of life's challenges was met.

Our prayers may not be answered the way we want them to be, but God is there for us. He truly wants us to trust Him, no matter how challenging or difficult things may be.

During all of these ups and downs, Ronald continued reading his Bible. In fact, just as a mental exercise, he would read portions of his Greek Bible, which he had taken two or three years of in requirement for a minor in Greek. This kept a line open with the divine Author of the Bible. This may be part of the way the Lord kept in touch with Ronald even though these were some of the most difficult times for him and his wife, times when they considered leaving the body of Christ, His church.

Fortunately, Ronald and Lily had the privilege of having several excellent pastors along the way. These were pastors who were true ministers of the gospel. They preached the Word from the pulpit; they encouraged them and visited them in their home. And more importantly, they prayed with Ronald and Lily. They were guides in a journey that still continues.

Binding

Even though they may not have been present when Ronald and Lily were tempted to the point of leaving the church, the memories of what these men and their wives said and did helped Ronald and Lily survive the rough parts of their Christian journey.

Similarly, good Christian friends have really been a blessing to Ronald and Lily. There have always been some who have supported them when they needed it. In turn, Ronald and Lily have also been able to do the same for others at different times. As they have helped others and others have helped them, a bond was formed that will last throughout eternity!

It was early on in Ronald's experience with Christ, that he learned that he could never stop returning the tithe. No matter how rough things got or how he felt about the church, Ronald remained faithful to God by returning his tithe. In Ronald and Lily's more than forty years of marriage, they have always paid their tithe. They also gave God their offerings. Whether they were in prosperity or adversity, in times of positive Christian experiences or times of disappointment and trials, they made sure that the Lord's portion of their income was always returned to Him. This also kept them linked to Him and His body.

By the same token, the Lord has been faithful to Ronald and Lily. They have seen Him work on their behalf many times over. When they married, they were still in college. But they received enough in monetary gifts from the wedding to pay for their tuition and rent for the first semester of their senior year in college. On two occasions during the first semester, they ran out of money and food. In answer to their prayer, a good Samaritan sent them some money, which they used for food, minus the tithe. Another time they received a belated cash wedding gift. Again they used the money for food and other necessities, minus the tithe.

Years later when they were both unemployed for a period of time, friends provided them with food. Their relatives have also been there for them in times of need, especially after returning from mission service in Peru.

Although Ronald and Lily did not grow up in Christian homes, they learned some positive lessons from their upbringing. Their parents worked long hours to feed and clothe their children. Despite being poor, they were kind and generous and shared what they had with others. Ronald and Lily never forgot these lessons, especially after

Binding

becoming Christians, and they have tried to practice these virtues in their lives as much as possible.

So it is that the grace of God is sufficient for each of us no matter how far away we may separate ourselves from Him. No one can change what has happened in the past, nor can anyone know what tomorrow will hold, much less the next second. Each of us can only live in the present, but we can always hope for a better life, now and eternally. Salvation is available for everyone. We can choose to accept or reject it. God will not force His will on us, just as Adam and Eve were not forced to obey Him.

It is the author's hope that all who have read this book will choose to accept and trust the Lord Jesus Christ as their Redeemer and Friend and live, not just for the present, but for eternity. This life is full of challenging situations and difficult choices. But we can be thankful we have the Lord by our side. Our journey in this life is short when compared to eternity. And the trials we endure on this earth will be worth it when Jesus returns and takes His faithful servants home to live in heaven and the new earth. If you haven't ever done so, read Revelation 21 for a glimpse into what the future holds.

We invite you to view the complete
selection of titles we publish at:

www.AspectBooks.com

Scan with your mobile
device to go directly
to our website.

Please write or email us your praises, reactions, or
thoughts about this or any other book we publish at:

ASPECT Books
www.ASPECTBooks.com

P.O. Box 954
Ringgold, GA 30736

info@AspectBooks.com

Aspect Books titles may be purchased in bulk for
educational, business, fund-raising, or sales promotional use.
For information, please e-mail

BulkSales@AspectBooks.com

Finally, if you are interested in seeing
your own book in print, please contact us at

publishing@AspectBooks.com

We would be happy to review your manuscript for free.

www.ingramcontent.com/pod-product-compliance
Lightning Source LLC
Chambersburg PA
CBHW020359170426
43200CB00005B/224